HEARST BOOKS
New York

An Imprint of Sterling Publishing
387 Park Avenue South
New York, NY 10016

ISBN 978-1-61837-116-4

Distributed in Canada by Sterling Publishing
c/o Canadian Manda Group, 165 Dufferin Street
Toronto, Ontario, Canada M6K 3H6
Distributed in the United Kingdom by GMC Distribution Services
Castle Place, 166 High Street, Lewes, East Sussex, England BN7 1XU
Distributed in Australia by Capricorn Link (Australia) Pty. Ltd.
P.O. Box 704, Windsor, NSW 2756, Australia

For information about custom editions, special sales, and premium and corporate purchases, please contact Sterling Special Sales at 800-805-5489 or specialsales@sterlingpublishing.com.

Manufactured in China

2 4 6 8 10 9 7 5 3 1

www.sterlingpublishing.com

HouseBeautiful

LIVING BY WATER

Lisa Cregan

HEARST BOOKS
New York

CONTENTS

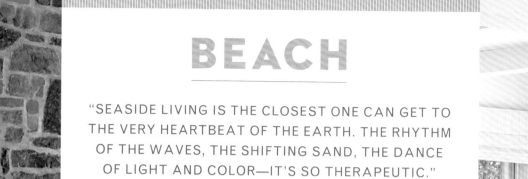

BEACH

"SEASIDE LIVING IS THE CLOSEST ONE CAN GET TO THE VERY HEARTBEAT OF THE EARTH. THE RHYTHM OF THE WAVES, THE SHIFTING SAND, THE DANCE OF LIGHT AND COLOR—IT'S SO THERAPEUTIC."

—CAROLYN ESPLEY-MILLER

See more of Espley-Miller's Carpinteria, California, house beginning on page 62. You'll fall in love!

SULLIVAN'S ISLAND, SOUTH CAROLINA

DESIGNER **SALLY MARKHAM** TAKES A CLASSIC OLD
BEACH HOUSE AND UPDATES IT WITH A FOCUS ON FAMILY.

"This great room is huge and wide open. The length of it looks out onto the sea. Yet it has all these seating areas, all these moments, so everyone in this large family can enjoy the space individually and still feel like they're together. The hide rug is soft, flat, cool to the touch, and quite stunning. Hide takes all kinds of abuse and is actually more divine when it wears down."

THE COFFEE TABLE'S FEMININE CURVES SOFTEN the squares of the rug. This Ellipse coffee table is from **Tucker Robbins** and the patchwork hide rug is from **Turabian & Sariyan.** 1950s slipper chairs flank the long, deep **Villa** sofa from **Holly Hunt.**

9

"This is a small, quaint town about 15 minutes outside Charleston. Totally relaxed, unflashy, family-friendly. Somebody's run-down home that's been in the family 100 years is right next door to a new one and this house has wonderful panoramic views of the Atlantic Ocean."

A POOLSIDE PERCH WITH A VIEW of the Atlantic Ocean. Cuba Lounge Chairs are from Mecox Gardens.

A LATTICE RAILING ON THE DAUGHTERS' BUNK BEDS IS A FEMININE TOUCH. The insides of the circles are painted Benjamin Moore's Peacock Blue.

"There are three girls in this family, and their room has bunk beds that sleep twelve because friends are always spending the night. There are six queen mattresses on those bunk beds!"

BRIGHT OUTDOOR FABRICS HAVE YOUTHFUL APPEAL on the screened porch off of the three daughters' shared bunkroom. The swing cushion is Nemo in Soleil by Manuel Canovas.

"THE FORMS RELATE, BUT THE
MATERIALS CONTRAST, SO YOU
GET HARMONY WITH TENSION,"
Markham says. A curved banquette, a
graceful round table, and slatted walnut
chairs "give the austere kitchen a more
organic feeling." Walls are banded in
24-by-6-inch Polar Plains subway tiles
from Urban Archaeology.

RATTAN PENDANTS LEND A BEACH-Y VIBE to the dining area. **O**rbita pendant lamps by **T**omoko Mizu are complemented by Gervasoni's **O**tto dining chairs of woven rawhide on ebonized wood.

"Using the same frames in different sizes makes it cohesive. Then we just hung them randomly on white walls. The ceiling fixtures are rectangles like the frames, so it's quite a strong space with all those lines and angles."

FAMILY PHOTOS IN MATCHING FRAMES ENLIVEN A NARROW HALLWAY and echo the black-painted window mullions in the living areas. Their firm lines are echoed in the shape of the ceiling lanterns from **CL** Sterling & Son.

ANATOMY OF THE GUEST ROOM

Designer SALLY MARKHAM

"This client urged me to use brighter colors than I normally would have, and I'm glad she did. They add excitement. This blue fur throw is absolutely drenched in color. On a yellow bed, it's the biggest contrast I could think of."

"The wall-to-wall headboard helps mask the fact that the window is off center, then I hung the large photograph for balance."

WHITE DOVE | BENJAMIN MOORE

"It's the South African in me that leads me to skins like this rug and the throw. There you're surrounded by so much game that it needs to be culled, so everyone has them. Fur is sexy and warm."

"I'm obsessed with symmetry and symmetrical layouts, which leads to a lot of lines and angles. I balance them with rounded shapes, like this tufting, because they're so feminine and calming. In my opinion, people lead much happier lives when there's femininity involved."

"I think white walls are always the right answer, but then again, I'm from South Africa, a country where it's almost always summer. In my houses, I tend to make a base of neutrals, and I use small amounts of color for contrast. I don't like too much color. It eats into the calm."

BRUSH FRINGE USED AS WELTING ON SOFA CUSHIONS IS FRESH AND FUN in the family room. Fringe is from **Samuel & Sons** and the big, bold ottoman is covered in **Nguni** cowhide. Vintage **Russel Wright** chairs are upholstered in Meloire Reverse by **China Seas**. **Calypso Home** floor pillows lend a cozy touch.

LYFORD CAY, BAHAMAS

DESIGNER **AMANDA LINDROTH'S** 1950s-ERA HOME IS
WHERE NEW ENGLAND PREPPY MEETS OLD HAVANA.

"You have shelves, and you lean the pictures. You just make it work. It has an insouciance, as if you might change or add things. You can't live in a purely resort house, with four shell prints in the living room. You need paintings and books, that layer of life. An island house should look like home."

IN THE LIVING ROOM, AN OPEN AND CASUAL ATTITUDE emanates partly from the leaning and overlapping pictures: "We collect paintings of the Bahamas from the late nineteenth to the early twentieth century by notable American artists who passed through here in the winters—but if our daughter, Eliza, draws something, it might land there, too." Adding to the ease is the Sunbrella stripe with which she dressed four 1960s armchairs that came with the house.

19

BACK STEPS, KEPT PRISTINE WHITE as if a canvas for bougainvillea, lead to the kitchen garden.

THE SALVAGED NORTH CAROLINA ANGLER'S BOAT docked outside Lindroth's house is used for one purpose: lunch. "We don't go far, we go slow, and we eat well," she says.

"The house had been lived in by one woman for a very long time, and I wanted to make it new. Out with the French château chandeliers and the fanciness. In with the sporty Sunbrella stripe."

FOR A BLANK WALL IN THE LIVING ROOM, LINDROTH SUMMONED 1960s BILLY BALDWIN and found a vintage rattan screen to fill the space—"super sporty." A console table is jazzed up with navy Island Ikat by China Seas.

A BLUE-AND-WHITE PALETTE keeps the library feeling cool and breezy.

CROWNING THE LIBRARY HEARTH ARE NINETEENTH-CENTURY WATERCOLORS of the Bahamas by Gaspard Le Marchant Tupper. Willow Group rattan chairs are pulled up to a backgammon table.

ANATOMY OF THE SUNROOM
Designer AMANDA LINDROTH

"The house had a terrazzo floor. And I didn't have the oomph to jackhammer it out. Seagrass seemed like a cozy remedy. I do it a lot. When you need to clean it, you replace it. Did you know seagrass is a dollar a square foot? It goes down, and if there's a problem, it comes up. Or we just hurl down one of those Dash and Albert cotton rugs, if a guest has spilled a glass of red wine on the seagrass, or if a dog or child has done worse. We have a stock of them on hand."

> "The sunroom is tented like a pleasure boat, a fun way to make it feel full of happiness."

"Teals and aquas can be misused, and turquoise is quicksand for the beginner. I'm more about royal and French and navy blues. I'm inclined to throw them all together and not to sweat it too much, not to tremble. Mostly, blues all fall together and do pretty well, especially navy and French blue."

LINEN WHITE | BENJAMIN MOORE

"I went to every junk shop in Florida and snapped up rattan swivel chairs and rattan peacock chairs and everything amusing about the midcentury resort moment that was also elegant."

> "Every island house needs a fantastic, spilling-over bar!"

"The fact that you see water from three sides—and the garden and the sky—was the biggest influence on the interior design. So the house is all white, in order not to compete. In the islands, white is like a uniform. But it's also a very American trait to use a lot of white paint."

"I love how the bold ikat on the two screens frames the dreamy eyelet bed and gives this low, 1950s room some architecture."

TO VISUALLY HEIGHTEN THE MASTER BEDROOM, Lindroth sheathed two ceiling-high screens in a **Duralee** overscale ikat print and brought the eyelet canopy as high as it could go. The **1950s Baker** console table, reglazed in a dark finish, holds a nineteenth-century English grotto mirror.

DAUGHTER ELIZA'S ROOM IS DECORATED TO GRACEFULLY TRANSITION from little girl to young lady.

MARIN COUNTY, CALIFORNIA

DESIGNERS **KIM DEMPSTER** AND **ERIN MARTIN** CREATE A CHIC POSTAGE STAMP OF A BEACH HOUSE THAT SOMEHOW COMFORTABLY SLEEPS TWELVE.

"This house is the right size for a family. People who have these huge houses never see one another. And when they do get together, they usually avoid the great room and sit in the breakfast nook. There's something magical about being in a small space. You don't feel lonely."
—ERIN MARTIN

"We're in coastal Marin, with a view of the ocean, and I've definitely got a nautical theme going. But we didn't want kitschy nautical. It's more marine industrial."
—KIM DEMPSTER

DUTCH DOORS AND HAND-CARVED DETAILING make this feel like "my Hansel and Gretel house," owner **Kim Dempster** says. The Victorian settee has been the site of many afternoon naps. When the picture window had to be replaced, designer **Erin Martin** saved the original to create a kind of shadowbox for a collection of sea-themed paintings found at flea markets and garage sales.

31

LEFT
THE HOUSE IS PERCHED ON A HILL, amid wildflowers.

OPPOSITE
A DECK AND GALVANIZED METAL JULIET BALCONIES on the upstairs bedrooms add to the square footage.

FROM THE PORCH, A BREATHTAKING VIEW of the wild **California** coast gives way to rolling whitecaps and the endless blue of the **Pacific.**

ANATOMY OF THE LIVING ROOM
Designers KIM DEMPSTER *and* ERIN MARTIN

"The ceiling is high and narrow, and the huge hanging buoy lights bring it down and create a kind of canopy. It's like putting a hat on the space."
—EM

"It would have been far easier to tear down the house, but we wanted to preserve the unique living room."
—KD

"I found that coffee table made from an old nautical chain in Erin's warehouse."
—KD

"And then I remembered I had a round piece of marble somewhere. It literally fit in the table like a glove. I thought, 'Yes! You two were supposed to meet long ago.'"
—EM

"This fireplace is my ode to Louise Nevelson. Our architect used to be a woodworker, and we got her to make it for us. When she said, 'I'm nervous,' I said, 'Just don't think. Let it put itself together.'" —EM

SNOW ON THE MOUNTAIN
BENJAMIN MOORE

"There's a sense of soul and spirit and nostalgia. There will be conversations around that fireplace for many years. It will evoke memories and create a history for this family, over time."
—EM

"I like big furniture in a small space. I might put as much stuff as I can into a small room, and in a bigger space, I'll do less stuff. There are no rules. Somewhere along the line we got stuck in a box. Let's get out of it and have some fun."
—EM

"When we first saw this place in 1997, it was paneled in the original redwood. It felt more like a mountain cabin than a beach house. We painted the interior white to make it light and airy."
—KD

AN ANTIQUE TRESTLE TABLE AND VINTAGE CAPTAIN'S CHAIRS in the dining area are illuminated by **Shaw** ceiling lights from the **Urban Electric Co.** A banquette, with more storage underneath, doubles as a guest bed. Vintage French linen—it reminds Dempster of sailcloth—hangs casually from **Restoration Hardware** rings at the window.

"The quotation by the dining room table says 'The pieces of a ship taken by themselves will sink. But when combined together, will take you anywhere you want to go.' For me, it's about family and loving one another, no matter what life brings you. It's something we know in our heart and our soul, but we need to be reminded occasionally."
—EM

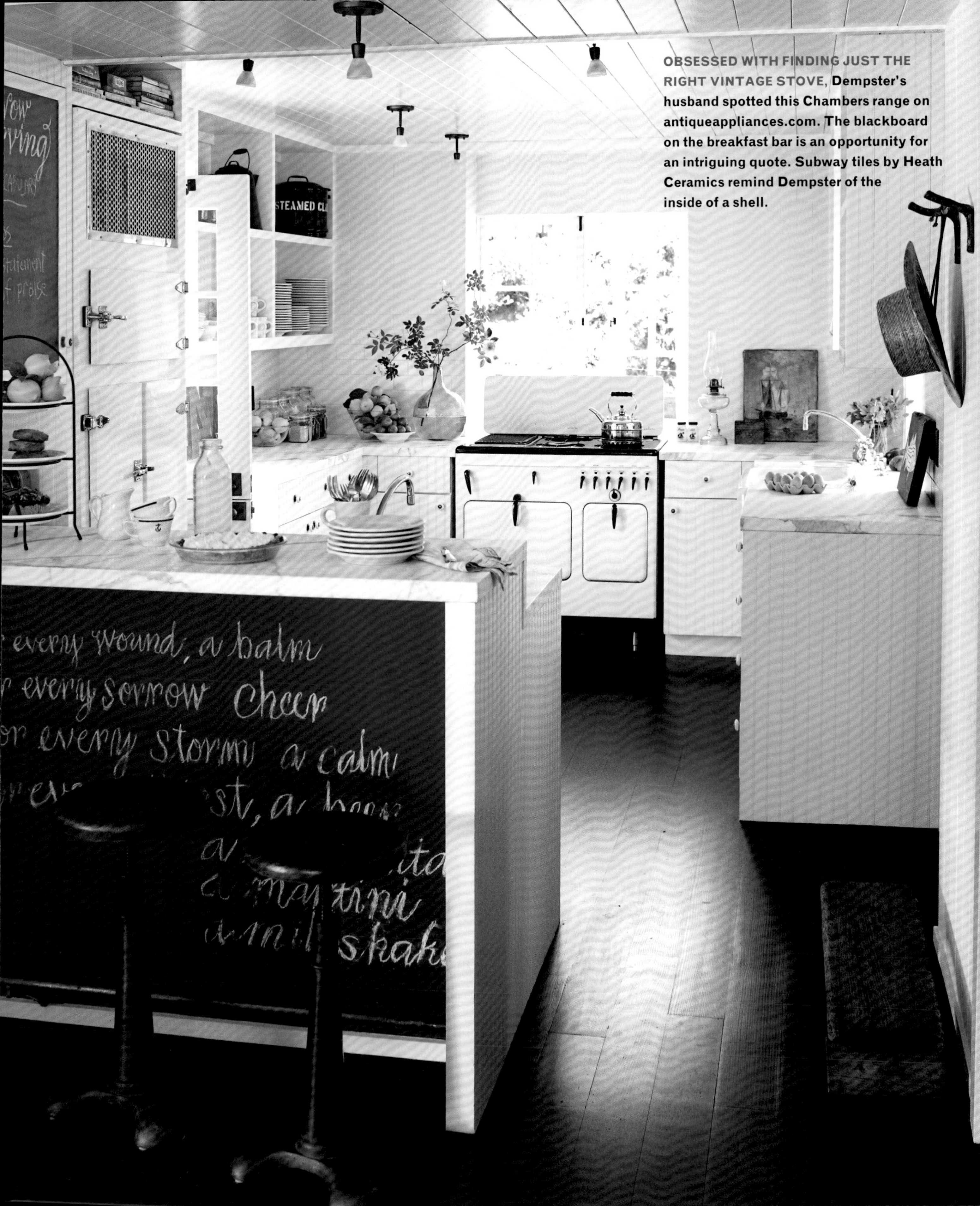

every wound, a balm
every sorrow, cheer
every storm, a calm

a martini
a milkshake

"Kids just love the bunkroom, and they'll hang out down there even when it's not bedtime. You have your own little compartment, and you can get in and close the curtains."

THE BUNKROOM MIMICS A SHIP'S CABIN and is lined with six bunks, four on one side and two on the other. Grommets on the curtains are meant to evoke bubbles. The brass porthole mirror was in **Dempster's** house when she was a child.

THE BUNKROOM BATH IS FITTED WITH LOCKERS for guests and family members. **Dempster** had the faucets on the **Kohler Brockway** sinks stripped down to the brass. The wall paneling is painted in alternating bands of flat and semigloss paint, echoing the stripe on the **Pottery Barn** towels.

CLOSET MIRRORS EXPAND THE SENSE OF SPACE in the master bedroom. The modern **CB2** platform bed is covered in vintage French linen, creating a compelling contrast.

THE HONED CALACATTA MARBLE COUNTER IN THE KITCHEN EXTENDS OUTSIDE to make passing food easier. Tolix Marais stools from Design Within Reach are pulled up to the counter.

THE SETTING IS THE STAR so the outdoor dining area is kept simple. An assortment of galvanized metal furniture—including Crate & Barrel's Lyle Side Chairs and 1934 Dining Chairs from the Sundance Catalog—is gathered around a table covered in Sundance's Americana tablecloth, made of homespun cotton and linen.

HAMPTONS, NEW YORK

DESIGNER **PODGE BUNE** CALLS ON FOND MEMORIES
OF HER ENGLISH CHILDHOOD TO CREATE A
SWEET ROSE-COVERED COTTAGE BY THE SEA.

"I found the fireplace on 1stdibs.com. It's old pine, carved with sea motifs, and it reminded me of one we used to have at the house where I grew up in England. I slathered the brick surround with cement and stuck stones from the beach into it. And the sofa's a wonderful French silk velvet—it used to be curtains I did for a client, who then got married to a very modern wife. So the curtains landed on my sofa, complete with that outrageous French bobbin trim."

"YOU HAVE TO HAVE A LITTLE BIT OF SYMMETRY— two mirrors, two lamps, two consoles. I found the consoles at an antiques mall. They're not a pair, but I ripped the tops off and put a piece of pink-and-white marble on both."

"THE TWO SMALL CHAIRS by the fireplace are boudoir chairs from about 1900, covered in an old Colefax and Fowler geranium print."

"THE EASY CHAIR is covered in my old dining room curtains!" Everything in the living room has a story.

43

THE STEPS DOWN TO THE BEACH
are marked with railings covered
in driftwood.

"I just nailed it on and
added a few shells. I
have to redo a bit every
year because the wind
takes it."

FOUR L.L. BEAN HAMMOCKS AMID THE TREES are very tempting on a lazy afternoon.

CACTUS FLOWER

BENJAMIN MOORE

GARDEN CUCUMBER

BENJAMIN MOORE

"On the vegetable garden's shed, Benjamin Moore's Garden Cucumber moves to the walls and Cactus Flower becomes the trim."

"Oh, if you'd seen it—
it was a generic 1970s gray
house with an asphalt roof
and Sheetrock walls, sort
of a cardboard box by the
sea. I thought pink would
be fun and whimsical
and mask the fact that the
house had absolutely no
redeeming architectural
features. I also added
more boards to the board-
and-batten to make it
a crisscross, and put on a
Hansel-and-Gretel
wood-shingled roof."

LEFT
REDOUTÉ PRINTS AND A TOUCH OF CHINOISERIE ADD COLOR to the master bedroom. **Coverlet by Calypso.**

BELOW
THE CABINETS IN THE MASTER BATHROOM WERE ORIGINALLY IN THE KITCHEN; Bune topped them with Carrara marble and fitted them with a Kohler sink. She forgot to measure before she left for an antiques show. Luckily, the mirror Bune found for the master bath just fit.

ANATOMY OF THE GREAT ROOM

Designer PODGE BUNE

"Lifting the ceiling meant more room for bookshelves and scrapbooks."

"I took down a wall and now it's basically one big room with the fireplace, the telly, the kitchen, and the dining area. The rest is just bedrooms. I've always wanted a house with one big room where everybody can do their own thing and nobody is left out."

"I love the plainness of the Corian island in the kitchen and it looks five inches thick with that edge. Counters do not need to be fancy."

"You mustn't overthink it. My house is a collaboration of things, either inherited or collected over a lifetime. It's eclectic. It's cluttered. I have done more modern things for clients, but that wonderful pared-down American simplicity of Halston or Calvin Klein is just not in my DNA."

"The dining chairs were plain brown wood, from a department store in London. I went to the Isabel O'Neil Studio in New York to learn how to do decorative finishes and painted those for my distressing class."

CUSTOM WHITE

"We added the tongue-and-groove paneling and the bead-board to the walls to make it feel more substantial, and then we painted everything white for freshness."

48

"I'll sit up there on that rock and look out at the water, and all's right with the world."

BUNE HAD THE TEAK DECK MADE WITH NO NAILS: "It makes the most incredible difference, especially when you're barefoot." The rock in the distance is crowned with a Buddha. A teak table and chairs from Patio.com is set with china Bune bought years ago at Habitat.

"I thought, 'Well, let's just have a riot in the garden.' I'm so bored with all white. But be warned. Roses are persnickety. I have to do a little nip and tuck every day."

ROSES INSIDE THE FRONT GATE WERE CHOSEN FOR THEIR SCENT—Bune didn't worry about color.

COASTAL MAINE

DESIGNER **TOM SCHEERER** PUTS A FRESH COAT OF
STYLE ON A GRAND OLD HOUSE WITHOUT FORSAKING ITS
DOWN EAST SENSE OF PLACE.

"That old Bar Harbor wicker that we bought down the road is like local produce, basically. It sets an informal tone, which is important. We do have some fancy upholstered pieces and fancy chintzes, and that wicker takes everything down. The combination is odd and unexpected but somehow works."

A DISPARATE MIX IN THE LIVING ROOM—antique wicker chairs, a Saarinen coffee table, and a Victorian-style sofa sit on a Moroccan rug from Shyam Ahuja. An ebony and gold-leafed Empire mirror hangs between curtains in Lee Jofa's Hollyhock chintz. For the sofa, Scheerer had Quadrille's Henriot Floral printed onto a sturdy cotton ticking, Malabar's Chetti Ticka.

53

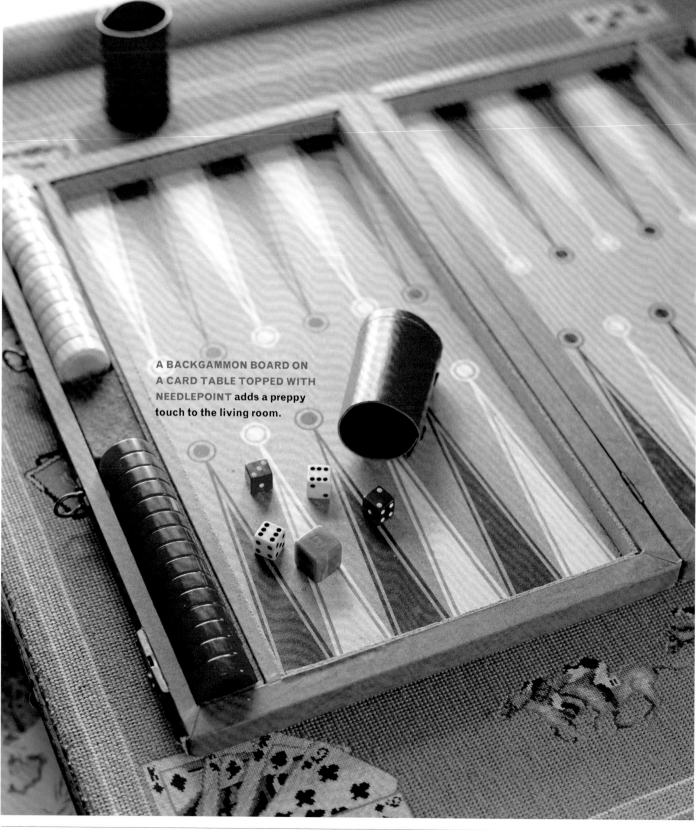

A BACKGAMMON BOARD ON A CARD TABLE TOPPED WITH NEEDLEPOINT adds a preppy touch to the living room.

ROUNDED SHAPES LEND SOFTNESS TO A SEATING AREA in the living room, a cozy blend of plush and informal. A vintage American basketball hoop takes center stage on a rattan scroll table, also vintage. The sofa is covered in Malabar's **Chetti Ticka.**

THE COLONIAL HOUSE SITS DIRECTLY ON SOMES SOUND. To make it look "more Maine," Scheerer shingled the exterior and changed the trim from white to Essex Green by Benjamin Moore.

SCHEERER ADDED A
PORCH TO THE HOUSE,
because "a summer house
shouldn't be porchless."
Skylights give it more light
on gray days. All-weather
wicker by Whitecraft.

ANATOMY OF THE DINING ROOM

Designer TOM SCHEERER

"A big, round table is only good for a crowd, but this square table is perfect for two or twelve."

"I hope it looks improvisational. At the same time, there was definitely a conscious effort to give it that layered house-for-the-generations kind of feeling."

"The walls are covered in a digital print of three paintings by Fitz Hugh Lane, a nineteenth-century Luminist. He painted a scenic view near the house. I pulled the images from books and had them scanned—I didn't have the nerve to call the museums. Then I sent the images to a digital artist, who forged them into a continuous scene. It doesn't read super-graphic at all—it really feels like the actual paintings."

"The dining table has a Formica top. I like Formica! It seems sort of normal. And it comes in good colors."

"It's a sixth sense for when to slow down, pull back. I don't like things that are overstyled. I've had clients who want more, more, more of everything, but I'd rather leave a job slightly underbaked."

"I think I was trying to channel the spirit of the grand summer houses of Northeast Harbor. The Rockefellers and Brooke Astor and a lot of the great lady decorators had houses there— Sister Parish decorated Mrs. Astor's house."

"I like to bring things to people that they haven't seen before. It's a little bit of a frontier, and it gets me into trouble sometimes. But I can't remember an instance when I had to give up, put it in the trash can, and start over."

A GUEST BEDROOM
HAS A DELIBERATELY
OLD-FASHIONED LOOK.
Wallpaper is Adam's Eden
by Carleton V. The chenille
candlewick bedspreads
are by Chelsea Textiles.

A LIBERAL ASSORTMENT
OF MIRRORS, PRINTS, and
sconces in the master bedroom
"offers an American version
of an English look."

TWIN BEDS IN A GIRL'S ROOM ARE COVERED in Botanical Fern by Schumacher. "I thought it was appropriate for a Maine house," Scheerer says. "It's a paradise of ferns here."

"The fern print is a very traditional print that's been used in country clubs for many years. It's an example of taking something very traditional and dowdy and making it a bit edgier by using it on a long headboard that holds two beds together."

CARPINTERIA, CALIFORNIA

DESIGNER **CAROLYN ESPLEY-MILLER'S** BEACH HOUSE
IS DEFINED BY POUNDING SURF OUTSIDE AND SHINING
WHITEWASH WITHIN.

"I painted the kitchen walls this soft soft seafoam green that feels like the color of the ocean."

A HANGING LIGHT WITH A VICTORIAN WICKER SHADE illuminates the kitchen table, which is made of antique corbels topped with glass.

A LARGE MIRROR OVER AN ANTIQUE FRENCH FOLDING TABLE gives the dining area the feel of a café in **Paris.**

"Show me a piece of campaign furniture that folds up or has handles and I'm someplace else. It speaks to me of far-flung travel and adventure and a lifestyle that's languid, sophisticated, and luxurious."

BARN DOORS WITH THEIR ORIGINAL SEAFOAM COLOR MAKE AN ARRESTING HEADBOARD in the master bedroom. Bedding is from Restoration Hardware; the blue accent pillows are vintage. Roses are from Espley-Miller's garden.

THE MASTER BEDROOM'S
MANTEL IS A WOODEN
FRENCH WINDOW FRAME
from Lucca Antiques. A framed
grid of shells on fishing wire
"sparkles and catches the
light from windows and the
fireplace," Espley-Miller
says. "It's so beautiful."

LAKE

"BLUE IS THE COLOR OF THE MAGNIFICENT LAKE OUTSIDE, AND IT WINDS ALL THROUGH THIS HOUSE. BLUE IS THE COMMON THREAD THAT HOLDS IT ALL TOGETHER, INSIDE AND OUT."

—MARTIN HORNER

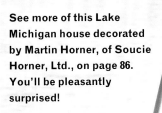

See more of this Lake
Michigan house decorated
by Martin Horner, of Soucie
Horner, Ltd., on page 86.
You'll be pleasantly
surprised!

LAKE LOTAWANA, MISSOURI

DESIGNER **RHODA BURLEY PAYNE** TURNS A SIMPLE 1940s FISHING COTTAGE INTO A COMFORTABLE FAMILY RETREAT.

"We wanted a color for the windows that would pop in contrast to the moss rock walls, that would add a lightheartedness. Blue just seemed right. Janet Curran, my client, likes purply blues, lavenders, so we went flip, flip, flip through a fan deck and started eliminating all the blues we didn't want, like royal blue, until we came to this periwinkle— Benjamin Moore Swiss Blue. Janet wanted very much to keep the integrity of what was once a simple little 1940s fishing cottage. The blue just seemed to feel at home."

OVERSCALE SHUTTERS IN THE COURTYARD HOLD THEIR OWN against the weight of the stone.

A WINDING PATH LEADS
to the lake.

"Do you know the word *gemütlichkeit*? It's German, and it means 'warm, cozy, friendly'—all the things this house is. A stone house with periwinkle blue windows and shutters ... everybody who passes by is charmed by it."

AT THIS PARTY-FRIENDLY HOUSE, the terrace overlooking the lake is a favorite place to entertain.

FRENCH DOORS OPEN FROM THE ENCLOSED PORCH to the terrace overlooking the lake—the doors "bring the outdoors in," Payne says.

OPPOSITE

"The draperies lend a softness and elegance to the room but the blues don't match the blue of the windows. The pillows on the sofas and the upholstery on the chairs are in completely different shades of blue too, and the background of the rug is aqua. But it all flows together. It's kind of a symphony of blues."

WHITE SOFAS THAT BRIGHTEN THE LIVING ROOM ARE DURABLE TOO, covered in **Donghia's** outdoor fabric, **Pinata**, and curtains are in **Vervain's Blythe**.

"I knew I needed to temper the masculinity of all the original dark pine paneling. So I began by putting two creamy white sofas in the living room. Then we did the ivory-and-blue linen draperies."

ANATOMY OF THE KITCHEN

Designer RHODA BURLEY PAYNE

"We did the cabinets in a green that blended, but didn't match the stove. And we did black tile for the hood to repeat the black of the cooktop," Payne says. "The cabinets are stained, not painted, so you see through the color a bit to the grain of the pine. The finish and the hardware give them a vintage look. Janet likes to have the hinges show, because that makes it look more authentically old."

DELFT BLUE TILE | COUNTRY FLOORS

"We did the tiles ceiling to floor—in a Wedgwood blue, a different blue from the periwinkle window."

"I had a client who wanted to use the same tiles but she was going to do it on just two walls. And I said it would be absolutely awful if you do it on two walls. You will have lost the impact of it. You don't do it halfway."

"The tile setter put the tiles up randomly. He instinctively knew not to put the same images of flowers next to each other. There are a lot of crooked lines, but that's all in the spirit of the original house. It was built in the 1940s and it was never meant to be anything special or fancy."

EVERGLADES | BENJAMIN MOORE

"Janet really wanted the Aga stove in pistachio but we thought 'What do you do to the rest of the room?' We thought about doing the cabinets in gray or brown, but that would just bring everything down. Then white, but, oh, ho-hum. Then it hit me: pistachio! It unified the whole kitchen."

THE DINING ROOM TABLE IS DRESSED with one of the dozens of colorful **April Cornell** tablecloths the owner has collected.

"We used the same vibrant Scalamandré chinoiserie in the master bedroom on the bed and at the windows."

THE SATURATED USE OF FABRIC PACKS A REAL PUNCH against the dark paneling.

"Every room in the house is so intimate. I think of this house as a place where you can be alone and feel like you have company. We shoehorned a large geranium-red sectional sofa into this small family room, for groups to relax on and watch a movie."

BAY HARBOR, MICHIGAN

DESIGNER **MARTIN HORNER**, OF SOUCIE HORNER,
FILLS A MIDWESTERN LAKE HOUSE WITH TREASURES FROM
AROUND THE WORLD, LENDING IT AN EXOTIC SPIRIT.

"In Michigan, people are expecting boats and buoys, and then they walk in and say, 'Wow.' Here are all these treasures—handwoven fabric, exotic tile, ebonized furniture inlaid with mother-of-pearl. It's as if the clients came back from a trip to the Orient with all these artifacts and incorporated them into the house. And it takes you on a journey as well."

"WE BUMPED OUT A BAY to create a real dining room and added the screens to define the living room from the dining room without dividing them."

THE DINING AREA HAS A VIEW OF LAKE MICHIGAN ON THREE SIDES. Curtains are Aegean Stripe by Cowtan & Tout. An Egyptian glass chandelier from Liza Sherman Antiques hangs above a table surrounded by a mix of chairs—a wood Charleston armchair by Richard Mulligan and Neptune chairs by Artistic Frame upholstered in Donghia's Angelina.

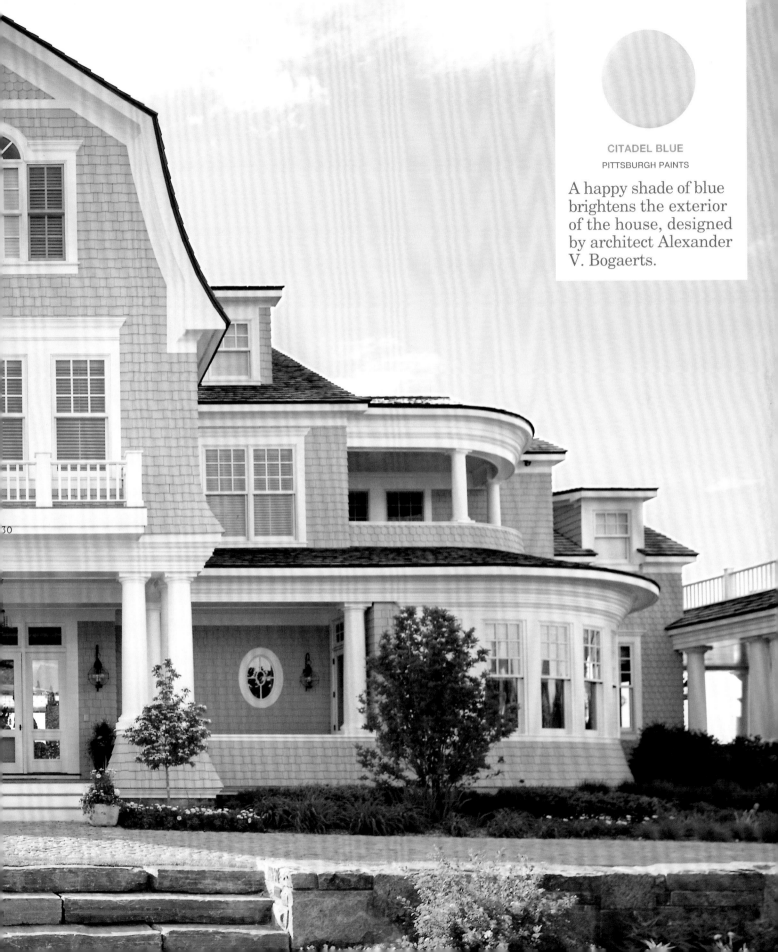

CITADEL BLUE
PITTSBURGH PAINTS

A happy shade of blue brightens the exterior of the house, designed by architect Alexander V. Bogaerts.

"We started with the living room fireplace—the focal point. We took three standard tile patterns and made a custom design out of them. I chose the paisley for the sofas because I liked its suggestion of India. It all draws you in. You want to touch all the fabrics and go over to the shelves and pick up one of the tramp art pieces."

THE LAYERING OF PATTERN STARTS WITH THE LIVING ROOM FIREPLACE, decorated with kaleidoscopic Moroccan tile from Urban Archaeology. Horner upholstered the sofas in not one, but two fabrics—Dedar's Sottosopra on the frame and Bergamo's Ucria on the cushions. Throw pillows made out of vintage textiles by Lynda O'Connor add more color. C&C Milano's Pienza Rafano covers the club chairs.

OPEN SHELVES FOR DISPLAY BREAK UP THE CABINETRY in the kitchen. Blue mercury-glass pendants from **Gallery L7** pick up the color theme. English sabre-leg counter stools are from the **Sterling Collection**. The backsplash from **Urban Archaeology** is both beautiful and practical.

THE KITCHEN HAS EXPANSIVE
VIEWS OF LAKE MICHIGAN.
**Two farmhouse sinks have an
old-fashioned look. The sink in the
island is from Rohl and the one by
the window is from Kallista.**

ANATOMY OF THE MASTER BEDROOM

Designer MARTIN HORNER

"I was in Morocco, and I fell under its spell. You walk down a street in Marrakech, and it's narrow and dusty—not beautiful at all—but push open a door, and you'll see amazing tile. That inspired me."

"The firebox was built a bit higher than normal off the floor so you can watch the fire from the bed."

PERSIAN PEAR
JOANNA ROCK
HANDPRINTED WALLPAPERS

MOROCCAN TILE
URBAN
ARCHAEOLOGY

"Mixing this tile fireplace with the intricate wallpaper is definitely a risk. I thought, 'Oh, my gosh, this is kind of crazy,' but I think it works because the blues in the wallpaper are as soft as the blues of the tile. And the scale of the patterns is similar. It's as if the tile and the wallpaper have the same value, in color and in texture. So they just blend into each other, in an easy, attractive way."

"As you travel through the room, your eye darts around to different objects. There's always something new to discover. You never get bored."

"One reason why you can have all this pattern and texture is because the palette is so consistent. This room is basically monochromatic. Everything is in shades of blue and cream."

A STUNNING WALL OF AZUL CIELO AND THASSOS MARBLE, cut with a water jet into a delicate Art Nouveau–like motif, is the focal point of the master bathroom. The pattern is Danse Azul by Artistic Tile. Etoile faucet and undermount tub by Waterworks.

SPARKLING ON A WALL IN THE MASTER BATHROOM, **tumbled Blue Celeste tile by Ann Sacks catches the light. The walnut cabinetry looks like furniture, not built-ins.**

SKANEATELES, NEW YORK

DESIGNER **THOM FILICIA** WAS LURED BY THE FADED
BEAUTY OF A DERELICT LAKE HOUSE, INSPIRED TO BUY IT
AND BRING IT BACK TO LIFE.

"I grew up nearby, in Syracuse, and we came here when I was a kid. My book on the house, *American Beauty*, is a little bit about going home and staying connected to where you're from and what you're about. It's also about the idea of not having to knock things down to make them relevant today. My house was built in 1917. I happened to see the 'For Sale' sign when I was up here for a wedding. I pulled in the driveway, and it looked like it was about to implode, it was so dilapidated. There were squirrels living in it! I thought, 'Ah, this house needs me. And I need this house.'"

A PORCH WAS ENCLOSED
TO CREATE THE SUNROOM.
V-groove paneling in Pittsburgh Paints' chic Black Magic sets off the rustic bark walls and the diaphanous Conrad Rain shades.

"When we have dinner parties, we light the fire pit—autumn, winter, spring, summer—just so you can see it from the house. Even on a hot night, people always end up gravitating toward it."

THE FIRE PIT, THE DOCK THAT EXTENDS OUT INTO LAKE SKANEATELES, and a Gerald DiGiusto 1960s steel sculpture.

A ROPE RAISES OR LOWERS THE LILLIAN AUGUST LANTERN above the patinated-steel dining table by the lake.

OPPOSITE

" The sofa is kind of ridiculously big, isn't it? I think it's ten feet long. It's called the Skaneateles sofa, and it's part of my furniture line—but not in that length. I made it that long for this house. "

THE LIVING ROOM'S SOFA HAS A LOW BACK, so it doesn't block views of the lake. Most of the furniture, fabrics, rugs, and curtain hardware in the living room are from Filicia's home collections for Vanguard, Kravet, Safavieh, and Classical Elements.

A LAYERED VIGNETTE IN THE LIVING ROOM STANDS OUT against walls in Phillip Jeffries grasscloth. Filicia's Strathmore console sits under *Warm Memories II*, a print from his Soicher Marin collection.

ANATOMY OF THE DINING ROOM

Designer THOM FILICIA

" My partner, Greg, and I have the entertaining thing in common. We like having lots of people around."

"The chairs are my Greek Peak chairs. They're named after the local ski resort!"

"Sound and lighting are very important to me when I entertain. There are built-in speakers hidden here, and every single light in the house is on a dimmer. I like the atmosphere to be soothing, and then around ten o'clock I might amp it up for fun."

"I wanted it to feel like a lake house, but also a home. Sophisticated, but also down-to-earth. Specific to where it is, but not a musty camp cliché. Younger, fresher. I designed the furniture, the rugs, the fabrics, the wall art, the curtain hardware. It's about as me as you can get here."

| BUCKLEY ROYAL LINEN | DOGWOOD BLOSSOM |
| KRAVET | PITTSBURGH PAINTS |

" The dining room does have an austere look, but the walls are upholstered, so the room feels warm and cozy. And it helps the acoustics. All the clinking and clanking of glasses and silverware doesn't reverberate and drown out conversation—dining rooms should be conducive to that."

"I love when things are restrained. I love when things are inspired by something fanciful, but they're dialed back. The idea of a reinvigorated, more relevant Americana excites me. I'm not looking to live in a Loire Valley château in upstate New York. If I wanted a château, I'd want to have it in France. Things should make sense for where they are."

"Bare floor, bare table in the dining room— I'm not big on tablecloths, to be honest."

HAVING ADMIRED DIAMOND-SHAPED WINDOWS IN STATELY OLD SYRACUSE HOUSES, Filicia introduced this one in the master bedroom: "I like how it floats in the wall." The window punctuates a screen wall between master bedroom and shower. On the bed, an orange duvet from Serena & Lily warms up a blue one from John Robshaw Textiles. The adjoining bathroom has twin Kohler vanities and Arhaus mirrors.

FLOODED WITH SUNLIGHT, THE MASTER BEDROOM'S SHOWER is "the next best thing to an out-door shower." Architectonics tiles from Waterworks line the walls.

"In the summertime, this boathouse is our waterfront home base."

BESIDES STORING TOWELS, WATER SKIS, AND LIFE PRESERVERS, THE BOATHOUSE SHELTERS A TOUCH PAD
for controlling music from dockside speakers. Inside, vintage chairs are grouped beneath a papier-mâché chandelier.
Come winter, the pavilion doubles as weatherproof stowage for the folding dock, paddleboards, and other gear.

OUTDOOR LIVING

"THERE'S NO REASON WHY YOUR
OUTDOOR SPACES SHOULDN'T BE AS LUXURIOUS
AND COMFORTABLE AS YOUR LIVING ROOM."
—MICHAEL S. SMITH

The inviting daybeds on this upstairs balcony in Santa Monica are from the Amalfi collection by **JANUS et Cie** and are covered in outdoor fabric from **Kravet**. The starry print on two of the pillows are the designer Michael S. Smith's **Star Atlantico** in **Ocean**, from **Jasper**.

"We wanted to give this courtyard an architectural presence. That's why we used these large, old window frames with mirror in them—which also make the space look bigger. The family entertains a lot after long days at the beach, so we added heated French lime-stone floors. Everyone takes their shoes off as soon as they get out there to warm up and get cozy."
—KATIE MAINE

"Everything here is meant to be a serene backdrop for the view. You can see the entire Austin skyline, and a chain of lakes."
—FERN SANTINI

"I think of this loggia as a part of the lawn. You step out and see fifty yards of lawn and palms swaying in the breeze, so the green on the cushions was a no-brainer."
—ALLISON PALADINO

"The houses all around share this lagoon off San Francisco Bay for pedal-boating, kayaking, small sailboats, and swimming. The large arched niche in the far wall is a shower designed to look like a fountain, and the basin is a hot tub disguised as a water element when not being used."
—PAUL WISEMAN

TO EVOKE AN ITALIAN PALAZZO, Wiseman used orange trees, a limestone terrace, and Amalfi lounges, table, and chairs from JANUS et Cie.

ANATOMY OF THE OUTDOOR LIVING ROOM
EAST HAMPTON, NEW YORK | *Designer* FRANCES SCHULTZ

"What proved to be the ideal cover for the patio was this framed, pitched roof with a canvas cover that can be put up in the spring and taken down in the fall."

"Budget-fatigued, I hung outdoor café lights for lighting. At times the simplest solutions really are the best ones."

"The metal settee, chairs, and ginormous pouf I'd bought ages ago at a tag sale are just right here, and the cushions are the very blue of my cottage's gates and shutters. Ditto with the color of the all-weather wicker chairs."

"My cottage is all about the garden, but sadly, there is precious little view of it from inside. A large porch opening onto it is the next best thing, and a covered, heated porch is even better. April through November, this is where I live."

"Consider outdoor heaters. Mine are propane-powered from Sunpak. They operate on timers and will dramatically extend the amount of time you can use your porch in the spring and fall."

"I knew I wanted a low, wraparound, enclosing wall that works as both seating and a surface for drinks or hors d'oeuvres. Sitting walls are a great feature. Build them to a comfortable sitting height—18 to 20 inches."

"Stacked stone walls define the space as an extension of the house but also become part of nature by incorporating planters and a fire pit," says designer Will Wick. Around the Aero dining table, designed by Wick for Restoration Hardware, are rattan chairs from Battersea. "Most outdoor furniture just misses when it comes to scale," Wick says. "These have the perfect amount of heft and a graceful curve on the back and the sides. They work everywhere."

ON DECK | OUTDOOR FIREPLACES

Designers create cozy outdoor fireplaces that warm both your feet and your heart.

RIGHT

WITH STONE THAT SEEMS CASUALLY STACKED and an ecclesiastical stone carving, this fireplace by architect **Robbin Hayne** has the look of a ruin someone happened upon in the woods. See how comfortably the huge rock nestles up to it?

BELOW

A ROUND SCULPTURE RESTING ON THE HEARTH ADDS FEMININE CURVES to the hard square lines of the fireplace. Designer Jean Larette chose orange for the cushions to echo the color of the sunset.

On a settee, playful pillows in a range of blues, chosen by designer Kristen Panitch, pick up one of the colors of the stones in the flagstone fireplace.

ABOVE LEFT

A BACKGROUND OF EVERGREENS AND THE GRIDLIKE PATTERN OF VARIEGATED STONE bring vibrant energy to this rectilinear fireplace. The outdoor room by designer Vicente Wolf is kitted out with deep sofas and filmy white curtains that filter light as they temper the architecture.

ABOVE RIGHT

AN OUTDOOR LOGGIA'S FIREPLACE is made of concrete embedded with stones, shells, and barnacles. "I've collected them from all over the world," homeowner Liza Pulitzer Calhoun says.

RIGHT

AN ART STUDIO MIRROR IS ATTACHED BY POLES BEHIND A STEEL FIREPLACE designed by landscape designer Jay Griffith, and artfully reflects the 1970s Venetian glass chandelier hanging from a tree. Stone balls that hide the gas jets are a chic touch.

THE SOARING HEIGHT OF THIS CONCRETE FIREPLACE by designer Pam Shamshiri gives it the feel of modern outdoor sculpture and its simplicity draws attention to the flames, lending intimacy and coziness.

OUTDOOR DINING

"I LOVE TO ENTERTAIN OUT HERE. WE'LL LAY OUT
CRABS AND SHRIMP ON THAT LONG TABLE, AND
WE GET THE BIG FANS GOING, AND IF THERE'S
MOONLIGHT YOU CAN SEE THE BOAT TRAFFIC ON
THE RIVER, SHRIMP BOATS COMING IN."

—ELIZABETH TYLER KENNEDY

As dusk approaches, the light softens at Elizabeth Tyler Kennedy's riverfront Georgia house.

"You feel as though you could be in Siena, except with a Weber barbecue."
—CHRIS BARRETT

A RUSTIC FRENCH BISTRO TABLE AND CHAIRS FROM INNER GARDENS GET VIVID SHOTS OF COLOR from linens designer and homeowner Chris Barrett purchased in Milan. Her terrace is made of pea gravel.

WITH ITS ROCK COLLECTION AND TREE-STUMP SEATS, the deck is low-key paradise. **O**chre's clean-lined dining table and bench are made of cedar from old Manhattan water towers, weathered to a soft gray. Homeowner **A**ndrew **C**orrie rigged a bamboo framework to support his homemade roof of lashed bamboo poles.

"The wisteria vines are over 100 years old. But the arbor was previously made of white wicker, so you couldn't see them when you were dining. Deborah Nevins, the landscape designer, designed an iron arbor to replace it."
—ROBIN BELL

THE TABLE'S MARBLE TOP WAS A MARBLE YARD CASTOFF, and Bell designed its iron base. Bell also designed the iron chandelier and hanging lanterns; both are inspired by streetlights she saw in Harbour Island, Bahamas.

FOR A SURPRISE, MISMATCHED CHAIRS chosen by designer Paul Siskin surround the dining table under a lakeside pergola.

ANATOMY OF THE OUTDOOR DINING ROOM
LOS ANGELES, CALIFORNIA | *Designer* MOISES ESQUENAZI

"I use the space under the deck for storage for outdoorsy things. I put everything related to entertaining—from barbecue tools to dishes, glassware, and plasticware—in big covered plastic bins."

"As much as possible I tried to treat it like an indoor room. So I've got speakers out here, and I've hung mirrors outside and put in good lighting, and lots of pillows. I also created a pulley system for little candle lanterns in the trees, so I just lower them and light the candles for parties."

"The backyard is meant to feel tropical and shady. The cushions and pillows add the color to the dark foliage background."

"The yard was grassy and all one level, so I put in a deck near the house, then created these different areas so it unfolds as you walk back toward the cabana. I put in a lot of plantings around the deck area. I wanted you to be in the house and see all these plants, and then to look beyond and see more garden and the dining area. That makes it look more expansive than seeing it all at once."

"This is where we entertain—big dinners, small parties. Our dining room is just too small. We have drinks up on a deck off the kitchen, then we'll have dinner at the dining table, then hang out afterwards in the cabana area."

FOR YEAR-ROUND COMFORT, designer Penelope Bianchi's loggia has radiant heat under its Mexican tile pavers.

PALM BEACH, FLORIDA

A JASMINE VINE CLIMBS THE WALL BETWEEN MIRRORED TRELLISES at this outdoor dining room. **Designer Mimi McMakin, of Kemble Interiors, sets the table with a classic Palm Beach pink and green palette.**

PASADENA, CALIFORNIA

CAMELLIAS ARCH OVER A TABLE draped with a **Clarence House Linen, Dahlia. Chairs are vintage French.**

"This is inspired by all the beachy towns in the Mediterranean, where alfresco dining is a way of life. I love the little village bistros with wild, rambling gardens and haphazardly set-up tables and iron chairs. I love having a meal among the wild and tangly vegetation of a garden."
—LINDSAY REID

"I'm not a fan of over-exuberant outdoor kitchens and barbecues. We intentionally made this one not so in-your-face."
—PAUL WISEMAN

ALFRESCO DINING INSPIRED BY THE COUNTRY THAT GAVE IT ITS NAME. The pergola contains a heating system and shelters an inlaid marble-topped dining table made in Italy for the owners.

ON DECK | OUTDOOR KITCHENS

Designers create alfresco kitchens so thoroughly equipped you'll wonder why chefs ever move indoors.

ABOVE

"The whole outdoor kitchen is wrapped in fieldstone and then we went for light-colored granite for countertops and pavers."
—KRIS HORIUCHI

ABOVE

THE U-SHAPED LAYOUT OF THIS NANTUCKET KITCHEN IS ZONED FROM HOT TO COLD, moving from the grill on the left to a pair of cooktops, the pizza oven, a sink, two refrigerator drawers, a beverage cooler, and an ice maker. Sink by Elkay. All of the other appliances and the stainless-steel cabinetry are by **Kalamazoo Outdoor Gourmet.**

LEFT

A STAINED WHITE-OAK CEILING POURS WARMTH over cool metal and a 16-foot-long marble bar designed by homeowner Bonnie Edelman. A drop-down metal gate protects appliances from rain.

THIS OUTDOOR KITCHEN TAKES ITS COLOR CUES FROM
THE EARTH AND THE SKY in California. Kalamazoo Bread Breaker Dual-
Fuel Built-in Hybrid Grill. "The huge chimneypiece is really just a design
statement, very French Château," says architect Michael Layne.

ABOVE
PLAIN & FANCY CABINETS AND BLUE-TONED CAESARSTONE COUNTERS PICK UP THE COLORS OF THE WATER just beyond the deck. Chandeliers from Kichler chosen by homeowner and designer Dianne Bernhard were antiqued with a metallic bronze finish. Paint on floor and ceiling is Benjamin Moore's Blue Springs.

LEFT
OUTDOOR KITCHEN CABINETS ARE MADE FROM OLD CYPRESS SHUTTERS at designer Malcolm James Kutner's Key West home.

OPPOSITE
"The walls aren't painted. Color was mixed into the concrete so the walls have a wonderful unevenness that looks hand done. And the ochre color is so vibrant, it reflects light back into the house and draws you outside."
—SANDY KOEPKE

POOLS

"I LOVE LOOKING AT MY POOL, THE WAY
IT'S ENLIVENED BY THE FLOATING SILVER BALLS.
WHEN THE WIND BLOWS THEM AROUND,
IT GIVES MOTION TO THE WATER."

—JAY GRIFFITH

At his Pacific Palisades pool, indigenous plants and sculptural plantings with very few flowers define landscape designer Jay Griffith's signature style.

SOUTHAMPTON, NEW YORK

CUSHIONS ON THE JANUS ET CIE POOL HOUSE FURNITURE MATCH THE CLEAR BLUE SKY and the ocean beyond at this seaside pool. They were chosen by designer **Kim Coleman.**

SONOMA, CALIFORNIA

DESIGNER STEPHEN SHUBEL hung striped outdoor curtains across the house's back porch and the front of the pool house to unify the buildings.

SANTA BARBARA, CALIFORNIA

LOW WALLS OF LOCAL STONE DEFINE THE EDGE between the formal pool area and the natural setting of ancient coastal oaks. Landscape architects Nolan Walmsley & Associates used an antique French limestone fountain to anchor the space.

CENTRAL VERMONT

AN INFINITY LIP makes it look as if you could swim right into the lake from the pool.

A GREEK TEMPLE FOLLY AT HIGHGROVE HOUSE, the country residence of Prince Charles, inspired the pool's wood pergola. Designer Brian McCarthy planned all the trees and shrubs on the property, which was once entirely alfalfa fields.

NAPLES, FLORIDA

DESIGNERS JESSE CARRIER AND MARA MILLER chose chaises with buttercup yellow Sunbrella cushions.

NAPLES, FLORIDA

"The pool house was a cavern before we installed the mirror. Now it reflects light and is so inviting."
—JESSE CARRIER

NAPA VALLEY, CALIFORNIA

AN UNDERWATER BENCH runs the length of the 45-foot pool, making it easier for designer **Ken Fulk's** dogs to get in or out, and for swimmers to lounge.

SANTA BARBARA, CALIFORNIA

THE LINES OF THE POOL AND ITS GRID OF STEPPERS IMPOSE GEOMETRIC ORDER on the unruly landscape that rolls to the sea.

ANATOMY OF THE SWIMMING POOL

WASSAIC, NEW YORK | *Designers* WENDY GOIDELL *and* CHRIS RAWLINGS

"The thing that ignited my interest was an article I read about natural swimming ponds, or pools. Clean, clear, no chemicals, no chlorine, aesthetically pleasing. There were all these magnificent stones on the property begging to be used." —WG

"The bridge stone took two of the biggest excavators I've ever seen to hoist and put on concrete piles."—WG

" I have to say, every time I swim in it, it's like being a child again. I grew up in rural New Jersey and swam in ponds. My sister said, 'You're trying to re-create that experience.'"

"It's clean, clear, and significantly healthier than a chlorinated pool. It makes use of the astonishing effectiveness of nature's ecosystems. Like any fresh body of water, it's colonized by microorganisms that purify and clarify it. They do the biological cleaning." —CR

"The bottom is lined with quarried round stones and perforated pipes that filter and circulate the water. The plants, of course, are part of the system, too. And as a precaution, we use ultra-violet light to eliminate any potentially harmful bacteria."—CR

"I had envisioned it away from the house. And then along came Chris Rawlings. He has a company in Massachusetts that builds natural swimming pools, and when he came to look things over, I pointed out where I thought the pool should go. He said, 'That's so far away. You won't feel connected to it.' As soon as he said it, I knew he was right." —WG

THE POOL PAVILION FURNITURE sports upholstery in **Perennials'** indoor-outdoor **Canvas Weave**, which is durable enough to hold up to homeowner **Liza Pulitzer Calhoun's** three dogs and wet swimsuits.

EAST HAMPTON, NEW YORK

A PAIR OF BIRD TOPIARIES INSPIRED BY THE GARDEN AT HIDCOTE, in England, perch poolside at Frances Schultz's weekend house.

EAST HAMPTON, NEW YORK

THE SWIMMING POOL'S CLEAN LINES HIGHLIGHT THE NATURAL CHARM of the lush hydrangeas and privet in the garden of a house decorated by **Robert Stilin.**

ON DECK | OUTDOOR SHOWERS

Designers know nothing says "vacation" like an outdoor shower.

THE SHOWER OPENS TO A PRIVATE OUTDOOR DECK in a California master bathroom by architect Mark Egerstrom.

A SHOWER IS SQUEEZED
INTO A ROCKY RAVINE
at a 1939 rehabilitated cottage
that sits by Lake Waramaug,
Connecticut, by architect
Gil Shafer. "It feels like
summer camp," Shafer says.

ABOVE

JUST OUTSIDE THE GLASS DOORS OF THE MASTER BATHROOM at a house in the Hamptons by Form Architecture is an alfresco shower. Protected on one side by a tall cast-concrete screen and on the other by a low wall of unfinished cedar, the space feels cool, yet sauna-like.

BELOW

THE DOORS ARE MADE FROM OLD CYPRESS SHUTTERS in the outdoor shower at designer Malcolm James Kutner's Key West, Florida, house.

OPPOSITE
The outdoor shower is more like a shower garden at a house by designer Douglas Durkin on the Kona Coast of Hawaii. It has a stacked lava wall and luxuriant tropical greenery. The towel rack design was based on batik drying racks used in Bali.

Christopher Baker: 128, 138 bottom, 154 bottom

Reed Davis: 4, 120 right, 121, 130 (both photos), 131, 139

Pieter Estersohn: 154 top

Don Freeman: 153

Mick Hales: 148, 149

Alec Hemer: 30–41

Ditte Isager/Edge Reps: 127

Francesco Lagnese: 42–61, 72–73, 86–97, 122 top right, 136 bottom, 138 top, 144–145, 150

David Duncan Livingston: 137

Thomas Loof: 8–17, 124–125

Jeff McNamara: 129, 143 bottom

James Merrell: 18–29, 74–85, 98–107, 142 top

Karyn R. Millet: 143 top

Amy Neunsinger: 123, 133 bottom right

Ngoc Minh Ngo: 112

Victoria Pearson: 110–111, 126, 132, 147 top

Eric Piasecki: 5, 113, 122 top left, 133 top, 146 (both photos), 155

Lisa Romerein: 122 bottom, 152

Jeremy Samuelson: 140–141

Annie Schlechter: 151 bottom

Tim Street-Porter: 114–115, 134–135

Trevor Tondro: 116, 117, 136 top, 151 top

Luca Trovato: 142 bottom, 147 bottom

David Tsay: 6–7, 62–71, 118–119

Jonny Valiant: 133 bottom left

Mikkel Vang: 108–109, 120 left

JACKET: David Tsay

FRONT COVER (clockwise from top left): Francesco Lagnese, Francesco Lagnese, David Tsay, Francesco Lagnese, Francesco Lagnese, Thomas Loof

SPINE (from top): Eric Piasecki, James Merrell, Reed Davis

BACK COVER (clockwise from top left): Mikkel Vang, Alec Hemer, James Merrell, Alec Hemer, Tim Street-Porter, James Merrell